GREAT
MOMENTS

What makes Manchester United one of the top teams in the Premiership? How have they outplayed many of the leading clubs in Europe? How can they take control of the game match after match after match? What makes them rock solid in defence, so strong in midfield and so dangerous in attack?

This book can't hope to give you all the answers – they'd fill an encyclopedia! What it does give you is pages of thrilling action, brilliant team moves and stunning goals from the last two seasons. From

Schmeichel in goal to Cole, Sheringham and Solskjaer up front, these moments of genius prove that Alex Ferguson's men keep playing world-class football season after season.

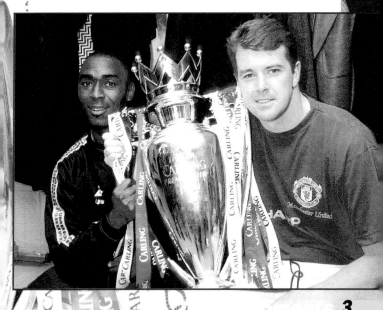

That Goal! • Th

Hero:
David Beckham

Date:
17 August 1996

Stadium:
Selhurst Park

Opponents:
Wimbledon

Competition:
Premiership

United began their 1996–97 Premiership run playing south London opponents Wimbledon. On a sunny summer afternoon Alex Ferguson's team showed their Championship form by defeating the home side 3–0. As if that was not impressive enough, the game will be perhaps most remembered for the dazzling goal scored by one of the Londoners on the pitch. It was not a Wimbledon player who caused the sensation, though. It was United's own London-born star – David Beckham.

The game went well for United, right from the kick-off. After 25 minutes, Eric Cantona smashed in the first goal and 33 minutes later Denis Irwin made it 2–0.

Then, right at the end of the game, with only seconds to go, David Beckham received the ball from Brian McClair inside

his own half. Looking up, he noticed that down at the other end of the pitch Neil Sullivan, the Wimbledon goalkeeper, was well off his line. From nearly 60 yards out, Beckham took careful aim and sent a perfect lob arcing towards the Wimbledon goal mouth. From the moment it left his boot it was heading like a heat-seeking missile straight for the Wimbledon net. Neil Sullivan was helpless as it dipped past him at the last minute and thudded in for goal number three.

The Premiership race was only 90 minutes old but already Alex Ferguson was calling this 'the goal of the season'. As for the players, Eric Cantona spoke for them all when he congratulated United's young hero with the simple comment, 'Beautiful goal, David'.

Hero:
Teddy
Sheringham

Date:
1 November
1997

Stadium: Old
Trafford

Opponents:
Sheffield
Wednesday

Competition:
Premiership

Manchester United began November 1997 as they had ended October, with another feast of goals. This time Sheffield Wednesday were on the receiving end of a United team hungry for victory. Teddy Sheringham, who had watched from the

bench as his team-mates put seven goals into the Barnsley net the week before, grabbed his share in this match.

Teddy opened the scoring after 13 minutes. He played a one-two with Ole Gunnar Solskjaer and then struck the ball into the net with the side of his foot from 20 yards out.

Seven minutes later,
Teddy helped Andy
Cole add to his total of goals for the season.
His pass bounced around between players
of both sides before Andy knocked it in for
the second goal. Andy also got the third.
Then Ole Gunnar Solskjaer joined in the
scoring with the fourth goal just on half time.

All three United strikers might have got hat
tricks against Wednesday. Teddy Sheringham

picked up his second goal of the match soon after the hour when he headed in a cross from David Beckham. And moments before the whistle blew to end the match he put the ball just wide of the net.

That left Andy Cole as United's only hat trick scorer in the season, but United still had a 6–1 win. Added to the score against Barnsley, Alex Ferguson's players had fired in 13 goals in two games in the space of seven days. This was also United's biggest ever win over Sheffield Wednesday.

Hero:
Ole Gunnar
Solskjaer

Date:
29 September
1996

Stadium:
Old Trafford

Opponents:
Tottenham
Hotspur

Competition:
Premiership

Just under 55,000 supporters saluted a
new United hero on this Sunday afternoon
at Old Trafford. For the first time since
joining the club, Ole Gunnar Solskjaer
played for all 90 minutes (having been
substituted by Andy Cole in the previous
game) and scored the only two goals
of the match.

He got the Old Trafford fans cheering eight
minutes into the game as he crashed in a

shot from the edge of the area. That was saved by Ian Walker in the Spurs goal. He came close 19 minutes later when he powered in a left-foot drive. Walker saved that shot too. But Ole Gunnar beat him completely in the 38th minute of the game.

Ryan Giggs floated in a perfect cross, Ole Gunnar gathered the ball and then paused for a split second to avoid Sol Campbell who was trying to block his shot. At the same time he sent Ian Walker diving to the ground just a fraction too early. With the

Tottenham goalkeeper already down Ole Gunnar steadied himself and coolly fired the ball into the net.

That first goal was a brilliant solo strike – his second came from a great team move. Jordi Cruyff and Eric Cantona built the attack as they switched play across the edge of the penalty area, wrong-footing the Spurs defence. Nicky Butt joined them to steer the ball to Ole Gunnar who used his instep to send the shot curling past Walker and into the net. From now onwards, Ole Gunnar Solskjaer had a new nickname – 'the baby-faced assassin'.

Hero: Roy Keane

Date:
23 November 1996

Stadium:
Riverside Stadium

Opponents:
Middlesbrough

Competition:
Premiership

Roy Keane's first goal of the season came from a superb team move by Manchester United. Ryan Giggs and the Neville brothers could not play

because of injuries so Alex Ferguson replaced them with Michael Clegg, John O'Kane and Ben Thornley for the game at Middlesbrough. All three young players slotted comfortably into the team and Roy Keane's goal in the 17th minute came from attacking play by one of them – Ben Thornley.

Ben had fired a shot at the Middlesbrough goal. This was deflected and was picked up by David May. David Beckham was out on the right wing, but Eric Cantona was coming in from the left and David May sent the ball out to him instead.

A Middlesbrough defender followed the ball to Cantona, but the United captain cleverly kept away from him as he looked round to choose his next move. Paul Scholes and Roy Keane were trying to make space for themselves in the box, but David Beckham was still unmarked on the edge of the area. Cantona spotted him and swivelled away from his marker so that he could send a pass over to Beckham.

By switching play to the other side, Cantona gave Keane and Scholes time to lose their markers. David Beckham kept up the pressure. He sent in a beautifully struck first-time volley which sailed across the six-yard box, where Roy Keane timed a perfect jump to head the ball past goalkeeper Gary Walsh. It was a goal any team would be proud of.

Hero:
Peter Schmeichel

Date:
4 December 1996

Stadium:
Ernst Happel

Opponents:
SK Rapid Wien

Competition:
Champions'
League

On a freezing winter
night in Vienna, capital
of Austria, United played
a brilliant attacking

game to win a place in the European Champions' League quarter finals for the first time in 27 years. Ryan Giggs opened the scoring after 24 minutes and Eric Cantona clinched a 2–0 victory in the 72nd minute. But the score-line and the team's performance might have been very different if it had not been for an amazing piece of play by Peter Schmeichel in the United goal mouth only 17 minutes into the game.

Although United had beaten Rapid Vienna 2–0 in the home leg, their other European performances that season had been patchy. They had lost twice to the Italian champions, Juventus, and once to Fenerbahce, champions of Turkey.

Against this background the away leg got off to a nervous start. The scoreboard was still showing 0–0 when Rapid's number 16, Krysztof Ratajczyk, crossed to Rene

Wagner right in front of the United goal. From point-blank range Wagner angled a firm downward header. Against almost any other goalkeeper it would have been a certain goal. Luckily for United Peter

Schmeichel is both athletic and tall. The mighty Dane flung himself to his right, reached down and then flipped the ball up and over the bar. It was a stunning save and it turned the game for United. Only seven minutes after the diving Dane had turned on his magic, Ryan Giggs cracked home the first goal in United's memorable win.

Hero:
Ole Gunnar
Solskjaer

Date:
12 January 1997

Stadium:
White Hart Lane

Opponents:
Tottenham
Hotspur

Competition:
Premiership

Ole Gunnar had already scored two goals against Spurs when United had played them at Old Trafford earlier in the season.

When they met this time it was again Ole Gunnar who led the United attack and got the first goal.

To begin with, Spurs had the better chances. One shot sailed just above the United goal seven minutes into the game. Two more smashed into the cross-bar, and Tottenham were still recovering from those misses when Ole Gunnar struck.

Roy Keane began the move when he sent Solskjaer a long pass from inside his own half. Ole Gunnar slipped the ball to Eric Cantona and then dashed between two Tottenham defenders. Cantona saw where he was heading and returned the ball for Ole Gunnar to run on to in the penalty area. As Ramon Vega raced in to close him down, Ole Gunnar drove a sliding shot from an almost impossible angle straight past the Tottenham goalkeeper, Ian Walker, and saw it fly into the net.

Two minutes afterwards Ole Gunnar set up a likely second goal when he delivered a pass that sent Ryan Giggs clear, but his shot went wide.

When the second goal did come, 14 minutes from the end of the game, it came with an unbeatable swerve from the boot of David Beckham.

Ole Gunnar remained United's top shot and in this game he sent a warning to every other Premiership side that he had plenty more goals to score in the season.

Hero: Andy Cole

Date:
5 November 1997

Stadium: De Kuip

Opponents: SC Feyenoord

Competition: Champions' League

In spite of his recent run of goals, Andy Cole seemed to feel he still had to prove to some people that he was a top European striker. The way he did this was to have his own fireworks party by scoring all three goals when United took on Feyenoord at home on Bonfire Night.

Andy and Ryan Giggs ran rings round the Feyenoord defence. His first goal came after half-an-hour's play when Teddy Sheringham let fly a blistering shot that the Dutch captain, Jerzy Dudek, did well to keep out of his goal. However, United won possession and Gary Neville lofted

the ball over the Dutch back line. Andy and Teddy raced in and just as the goalkeeper reached for the ball, Andy lifted it over him and into the net with his outstretched foot.

Just before half time Teddy helped David Beckham open up the right-hand side of the field. Teddy's pass let David send over a cross for Andy to tap in the second goal with the side of his foot.

Andy's third goal came from a great team move. After some careful midfield play Gary Pallister led the attack and sent a perfect pass right through the Feyenoord defence for Ryan Giggs. Ryan's speed and Gary's quick thinking left them standing. Ryan slipped round the goalkeeper and whipped the ball back from the by-line before it went out of play. Once again Andy Cole was in just the right place and slipped the ball into the open goal.

**Hero:
David May**

**Date: 5
March 1997**

**Stadium:
Old Trafford**

Opponents: FC Porto

Competition: Champions' League

The goal David May scored against the Portuguese champions set up United for one of their most memorable European victories.

Porto came to Old Trafford with a fearsome reputation. Newspapers were calling them the second most powerful club in the competition. They had already won all their away matches in the league section and United knew they would have to play at their very best to defeat them at Old Trafford.

On the night they did just that.

Alex Ferguson's team played brilliantly after Porto had broken through down the right and sent in a dangerous cross in the first two minutes. United didn't give them a chance for the rest of the game. They won corners and free-kicks that kept testing Hilario, the Porto goalkeeper.

But it took 22 minutes for the goals to come and when they did it was David May who got the first.

David Beckham lofted in a cross towards Gary Pallister and David May. Pallister got to the ball but the goalkeeper knocked away his header. In the goalmouth struggle David May was on the ground when the ball fell to him. Even so he managed to reach out a foot and knock it into the Porto net.

It may not have been the most powerful goal David May has scored, but it was certainly one of the most important. For the rest of the game, United ran rings round the Portuguese team and put three more goals past them to clinch a brilliant 4–0 win.

Hero: Gary Pallister

Date: 19 April 1997

Stadium: Anfield

Opponents: Liverpool

Competition: Premiership

Manchester United won a convincing victory over Premiership rivals Liverpool when they beat them 3–1 at Anfield. And in beating Liverpool in such confident style United set themselves up for their fourth Premier League title in five years.

The match kicked off at 11.15 am and 15 minutes later United won a corner, taken by David Beckham. He curled in a perfect cross and waiting to head it into the Liverpool goal was Gary Pallister. Leaping high above his marker, he powered the ball into the top corner of the net, far from the reach of David James, the Liverpool goalkeeper.

When he wasn't scoring Gary Pallister was working with Ronny Johnsen to stop Liverpool moves that looked like getting anywhere near the United goal. Throughout the first half United successfully closed down the Liverpool strikers.

However John Barnes got one back for the home team to make the score 1–1. But United were always in control of the game and just before half time they struck again.

David Beckham curled in a corner and Gary Pallister again beat his marker to head in goal number two. That was the goal that convinced many United supporters that

they would be the Premiership Champions once more.

In the second half Liverpool tried different tactics. They played long balls into the United penalty box, but the United defence and Gary Pallister in particular were always in place to win possession. When Andy Cole scored United's third goal Liverpool ran out of ideas.

Hero:
Gary Neville

Date: 5 May
1997

Stadium:
Old Trafford

Opponents:
Middlesbrough

Competition:
Premiership

The rain poured down
and the goals poured
in in this exciting
match. The pitch was
so wet that players in

both teams slipped and slid as they tried to keep control of the ball. Two days earlier United had drawn a hard match 2–2 with Leicester after trailing 2–0. Now they soon found themselves two goals behind against Middlesbrough.

Juninho put Middlesbrough ahead after 15 minutes. Twenty minutes later Andy Cole had a shot blocked at the other end of the pitch. But

his effort bounced back to the feet of Roy Keane who hammered in an equaliser.

Middlesbrough hit back almost immediately with two quick goals from Emerson and Hignett. As half time approached United were 3–1 down and struggling – especially in defence.

Then one of the defenders who was being given such a hard time by the Middlesbrough strikers showed why Manchester United deserved the Premier League trophy. Gary Neville had never scored for the first team, but in the wet and mud of his home stadium he took his chance. Racing on to a pass from Eric Cantona, Gary drove the ball into the far corner of the goal with all the power and confidence of a full-time centre forward.

By scoring just before the half-time whistle Gary Neville gave his team the boost they needed. Middlesbrough's well of goals dried up in the second half and Gary rounded off the game by sending in the cross that Ole Gunnar Solskjaer headed in to draw the game 3–3.

Crowning Glo[ry]

Hero:
Ole Gunnar Solskjaer

Date: 11 May 1997

Stadium: Old Trafford

Opponents: West Ham United

Competition: Premiership

Manchester United already knew that they were the 1999–97 Premier League Champions when they played this last match of the season. It was fitting that Ole Gunnar Solskjaer, the season's great find, helped in scoring the goal that put United in front.

One year earlier few United supporters had ever heard of Ole Gunnar Solskjaer, but in his first season the Norwegian striker had become the team's top scorer and a big favourite with supporters.

Twelve minutes into the game United won a corner and David Beckham stepped up to take it. His kick curled in and finally dropped to Paul Scholes. From outside the area Paul cracked in a blistering shot which

hammered into the underside of the cross-bar before bouncing over the line. He had hit his shot with such force that no one could be sure what had happened. Had he scored, or hadn't he?

Luckily for United, Ole Gunnar Solskjaer reacted with the same brilliant quick-thinking that had produced so many of his goals. Leaping into the air, he managed to reach the ball as it bounced up from the goal line and headed it into the net. There was no mistaking this – United were ahead. Victory was assured when Jordi Cruyff scored the last goal of the season to make it 2–0.

Hero: Denis Irwin

Date: 17 September 1997

Stadium: Lokomotiva

Opponents: FC Kosice

Competition: Champions' League

In their first Champions' League match of 1997–98 United travelled to Slovakia to take on the Slovak champions, Kosice. They came away after scoring three goals and keeping a clean sheet – their best start to a European competition for several years.

For the United defenders it was a special night to remember as two of their number fired in the first two goals. Denis Irwin had particular reasons to feel pleased with his first European game of the season.

Ryan Giggs was unable to play against Kosice which meant that right from the kick-off Irwin had to defend the left side of the field from the attacking runs of the

Kosice captain, Ivan Kozak, without Ryan's help. A player with less experience might have let Kozak slip through, but Denis marked him well and after half-an-hour got his own back.

He made a deep run, bursting through into the Kosice half, and got behind their defence where he received a pass from

Andy Cole. Once again, Denis's experience showed. After checking to see whether any team-mates were in a better position to score, he decided to shoot. He then fired a low shot under the goalkeeper's body to score his very first European goal.

Then, just over 30 minutes later, Henning Berg scored his first goal for United when he smashed in a David Beckham free-kick. And two minutes before the end of the match Andy Cole rounded off a triumphant win with the third goal of the night.

Hero:
Ryan Giggs

Date:
1 October 1997

Stadium:
Old Trafford

Opponents:
Juventus

Competition:
Champions'
League

When Manchester
United had played
Juventus in the
previous season,

Giggs In Gear

they had lost both matches. But Manchester United had come a long way since then and when they met at Old Trafford for this game United were determined to win.

This determination was made even stronger after Juventus snatched an early goal inside the first minute of the game. United stayed calm, however. They kept the ball away from the Italians, looked for chances and got their reward 36 minutes later. Ryan

Giggs In Gear

Giggs, who had been slicing his way through the Juventus defence with ease, broke away down the wing and then sent over a high cross. Teddy Sheringham was there to meet it in front of the Juventus goal and he angled in a powerful downward header towards the far post. This beat the goalkeeper and two defenders and drew United level, 1–1.

Paul Scholes gave United the lead after 69 minutes when he sent the Juventus goalkeeper the wrong way before scoring the second goal.

Twenty minutes later it was Ryan's own turn to score. The Juventus defence had no answer to his penetrating run when he raced on to a perfect pass from Teddy Sheringham, sprinted towards the goal and powered a shot into the roof of the net. It was a brilliant goal, perhaps one of the best he has ever scored.

Even though Juventus scored again right at the end of the game, no one could wonder why Manchester United now moved alongside them as joint favourites for the European Cup.

Hero: Paul Scholes

Date: 22 October 1997

Stadium: Old Trafford

Opponents: SC Feyenoord

Competition: Champions' League

Double Dutch

Manchester United's unbroken run in the 1997–98 Champions' League continued when they took on the Dutch champions Feyenoord at Old Trafford and beat them 2–1.

When their two goals from this match were added to those they had already scored, United's goal total was already higher than it had been from all the previous season's group matches in the Champions' League.

The United score might have been higher against Feyenoord if chances for Andy Cole and Ryan Giggs had not been well saved by Jerzy Dudek in goal. Like Peter Schmeichel at the opposite end of the pitch, Dudek

Double Dutch

was also captain of his side and for the first half-hour he kept his team in the match.

In the 32nd minute Denis Irwin crossed the ball to Andy Cole, and he knocked it down cleverly to the feet of Paul Scholes. Paul, who had already got his brilliant goal against Juventus, now scored with another superb strike against Feyenoord. Using a delicate flick, he sent the ball curling off the outside of his right boot into the Dutch team's goal. Lightning-quick reactions, perfect balance and world-class ball control came together to put United in the lead – and they all belonged to Paul Scholes.

Double Dutch

Denis Irwin put United 2–0 up 40 minutes later when he slammed in a penalty won by Teddy Sheringham. This was the first time Denis had taken a penalty for United since May 1995, but his spot-kick skills were as sharp as ever and Dudek had no chance.

Hero: Andy Cole

Date: 25 October 1997

Stadium: Old Trafford

Opponents: Barnsley

Competition: Premiership

Although United had beaten Feyenoord 2–1 four days earlier, Alex Ferguson and his team were worried by the number of missed chances. Among the strikers Andy Cole was determined to make the most of every opportunity and the rest of the team followed his example. It was unlucky for Barnsley that they were the victims of this all-out attack which ended with a thumping 7–0 win for Alex Ferguson's team.

Andy Cole scored three of the goals, making him the first United player to score a hat-trick in three-and-a-half years.

His first came after 17 minutes play when he pounced on a weak pass from Darren Sheridan. Cole stole the ball from Arjan De Zeeuw, slipped past the Dutchman and powered in the opening goal.

Two minutes later it was Andy again, this time gathering a pass from Ole Gunnar Solskjaer and burying it in the net without a moment's hesitation.

Ryan Giggs scored the third goal and right on half time he set up Andy for his hat trick. Andy raced through to collect a perfectly struck pass from Ryan which took him clear of the Barnsley back line. After already scoring two goals in the match, he made no mistake with his third and sent the ball curling over the Barnsley goalkeeper to give United a 4–0 lead.

Three more goals followed in the second half and Andy Cole was there to create the last, when he broke through to let Karel Poborsky back-heel goal number seven.

Hero:
Ole Gunnar
Solskjaer

Date:
25
September
1996

Stadium:
Old Trafford

Opponents:
SK Rapid
Wien

Competition: Champions' League

This was United's first home match in the 1996–97 Champions League. Two weeks earlier Alex Ferguson's team had played away against Juventus, the reigning champions of Italy and Europe. That match ended 1–0 to the Italians, but the score-line flattered United. Juventus had totally outplayed them. After that shock United ran out against the Austrian side determined to show who was boss, helped on by their Old Trafford supporters.

Although Ole Gunnar Solskjaer was making his first European start for United in this match, he showed no sign of being nervous. Just a minute after kick-off he fired a snap shot that thudded into the side-netting.

Solskjaer was in action three minutes later when he took the ball on the run and let fly another powerful drive. Two more chances soon followed.

Ole Gunnar was finally rewarded with his first European goal after a careful build-up

which started with Denis Irwin. From the centre circle, Denis hit a long pass to the edge of the area where it reached David Beckham. Beckham swivelled away from a defender and stroked the ball wide to Roy Keane on the right who cracked in a

low cross that just missed Karel Poborsky's
outstretched foot. But Solskjaer had read
the move so quickly that he slipped in at
the

far post
to steer
the ball
into the
net. Six
minutes
later David
Beckham
powered
home a
second
goal and

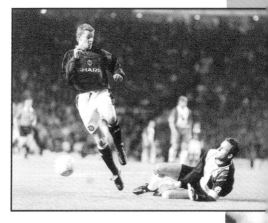

United were right back on track in their
European challenge.

Hero:
David Beckham

Date:
22 February
1997

Stadium:
Stamford Bridge

Opponents:
Chelsea

Competition:
Premiership

After defeating Arsenal 2–1 in a hard match at Highbury only three days earlier, United took on Chelsea at Stamford Bridge and found themselves a goal down after just three minutes. The scorer was Chelsea's brilliant Italian striker, Gianfranco Zola. He slipped past Denis Irwin and Gary Pallister and then totally wrong-footed Peter Schmeichel as he drove the ball into the United net.

Zola continued causing problems throughout the first half of the match.

However, United stood firm and began to win control of the game in the second half. Gary Pallister and Ronny Johnsen worked tirelessly to stop Zola setting up any more chances. Alex Ferguson's team pushed play forwards and began sending in crosses that kept on beating the Chelsea defence.

Sixty-eight minutes into the match Gary Neville began another United attack by running powerfully towards the Chelsea defenders and then sending in another well-struck cross. Chelsea's Frank Sinclair tried to head it away, but the ball flew high into the air and then dropped towards David Beckham.

From 12 yards out he watched the ball carefully as it fell towards him and then volleyed it with all his power. Chelsea's substitute goalkeeper, Frode Grodas, could only stand and watch as the ball flashed past him into the roof of the net. David had kicked it so hard that his equaliser was measured at a speed of 97.9 mph!

Hero:
Teddy Sheringham

Date:
9 November 1997

Stadium: Highbury

Opponents: Arsenal

Competition:
Premiership

The newspapers called this clash between Arsenal and Manchester United the biggest Premiership game played so far in the 1997–98 season. It proved to be a very big game for Teddy Sheringham who scored two goals in 13 minutes to level the score after United found themselves trailing 2–0.

Arsenal scored two goals in the first half-hour, but United didn't panic. They stayed calm and looked for chances, and Teddy's first goal came six minutes after Arsenal had celebrated their second.

Gary Neville provided the cross. Teddy found a huge gap in the Arsenal defence and headed the ball past his England team-mate David Seaman.

Seven minutes later he beat Seaman again. This time Ryan Giggs slipped the ball to him. Teddy nipped round a defender and cracked in the equaliser before Seaman had time to react.

Then came half time. Arsenal had been shaken by Teddy's swift reply to their first-half lead. When they came out for the second half, they lined up a three-man defence against United. This meant there was an extra player in midfield to stop Teddy getting a hat trick.

David Platt gave Arsenal a 3–2 victory with a winning goal in the 83rd minute, but United had shown that they had the fight and the determination to pull back from a losing position, even against the toughest teams in the Premiership.

Hero: Ole Gunnar Solskjaer

Date: 30 November 1997

Stadium: Old Trafford

Opponents: Blackburn Rovers

Competition: Premiership

Although Ole Gunnar had not started a game in four matches until United met Blackburn on the last day of November, he looked as sharp as ever.

A week earlier Blackburn had been second in the Premiership,

only a point behind United. As they walked off the field at the end of this match the gap had widened to four points, Chelsea had replaced them in second place and two of the goals in United's 4–0 win had been Blackburn own goals! The other two had been scored by Ole Gunnar.

He got his first when the game had been going for 17 minutes. After breaking through the Blackburn defence, Ole Gunnar played a neat one-two with Teddy Sheringham. Then he brought the ball under control from chest height, raced past a defender and fired the ball past goalkeeper Tim Flowers.

There was no way back for Blackburn after that early strike. Playing on the left, Ole Gunnar kept slicing through the Blackburn defence and seven minutes after the start of the second half he locked on to another flick from Teddy Sheringham, beat his marker and steered the ball past Flowers to score his second goal.

Blackburn had one chance that was well saved by Peter Schmeichel, but apart from that the second half was a nightmare for them. Sutton was sent off, Henchoz scored the first own goal and six minutes from the end of the game Kenna scored the second own goal after another Solskjaer strike.

Hero: Ryan Giggs

Date:
15 December 1997

Stadium:
Old Trafford

Opponents:
Aston Villa

Competition:
Premiership

Until this match Aston Villa had not let United score against them at Old Trafford for nearly three years. When they did score in the second half of this match it was the unstoppable Ryan Giggs who got the goal.

Ryan had chances to score in the first half of the game. A pass from Gary Neville gave him a shot at the far post, which the goalkeeper, Michael Oakes, did well to save.

Solskjaer and Sheringham also had chances saved by Oakes. Then Ryan hit another screamer that Oakes fumbled as it bounced away from his hands.

A couple of minutes later Ryan was in the attack again, this time sending a header over the cross-bar.

Villa went off at half time knowing that

more was to follow after the break. In fact, Michael Oakes came out early to go through his routine in goal before the

second half kicked off.

Ryan Giggs was soon back in action following up an attacking move that started with Peter Schmeichel.

The United captain sent a clearance up field that found Teddy Sheringham. He flicked the ball on to Andy Cole who showed tremendous skill in lifting it over Ugo Ehiogu so that it came down perfectly

for Ryan as he
raced through
towards the
goal. Ryan took
the ball on the
volley and sent
it through the
goalkeeper's
legs into
the net.

It had taken four
United players
just ten seconds
to move the ball
from their own
goal area into
the back of
Villa's net.

Hero:
Peter Schmeichel

Date:
21 December 1997

Stadium:
St James' Park

Opponents:
Newcastle United

Competition:
Premiership

In their last match before Christmas, United travelled to Newcastle where they had been soundly beaten 5–0 the season before. They might have lost again in this match if it had not been for the unbeatable play of their captain and goalkeeper, Peter Schmeichel.

United had chances, but Newcastle had more. John Barnes and Stuart Pearce both came close to scoring for Newcastle and it was only the brilliance of Peter Schmeichel that kept United's sheet clean.

Then Newcastle had a free kick 67 minutes into the game, taken by Stuart Pearce. His cross was safely cleared by Ronny Johnsen. The ball found its way to David Beckham who spotted Andy Cole in front of the Newcastle goal. David's cross let Andy jump clear of his marker to score with a sizzling header. United were 1–0 ahead and that is how the score remained.

Newcastle kept up the pressure but they could not get past Peter Schmeichel that afternoon. He played a true captain's game and when his team went home to enjoy Christmas they were four points clear of their nearest rivals at the top of the Premiership.

Hero: Andy Cole

Date:
4 January 1998

Stadium:
Stamford Bridge

Opponents:
Chelsea

Competition:
FA Cup

For their first match of 1998 United took on the Cup holders Chelsea in this FA Cup clash at Stamford Bridge. Both teams played all out to

win but it was United who came away with a crushing 5–3 victory.

Ronny Johnsen, Andy Cole and Paul Scholes came close to scoring in the first 20 minutes before clever play by Andy Cole got the ball to Teddy Sheringham, who set it up for David Beckham to crack in the opener.

A foul on Ryan Giggs five minutes later gave Beckham his second chance when he curled a free kick round the

Chelsea wall, beating Ed de Goey in goal.

Play had moved into first-half injury time when Ryan Giggs sliced through the Chelsea defence sending a pass down the left for Andy Cole. Chelsea defenders, tried to get back but Andy was too quick for them. With only the goalkeeper to beat he steadied himself, waited for de Goey to move forwards and then chipped the ball over him to score.

There was no let-up in the early part of the second half. Nicky Butt, who had dominated the midfield, won the ball again for United. The attack built as the ball was worked out to Ryan Giggs. Once again he sent an excellent through-ball for Andy, who held off a Chelsea defender as he steered a left-foot shot through de Goey's legs for his second goal of the match, his nineteenth of the season and his fiftieth for Manchester United.

Hero: Philip Neville

Date: 28 February 1998

Stadium: Stamford Bridge

Opponents: Chelsea

Competition: Premiership

Eight weeks after booting Chelsea out of the FA Cup with their 5–3 win, United returned to Stamford Bridge for this Premiership match. Phil Neville had missed out on the Cup game because of suspension. He was also the only United player on the pitch who had not scored for the club in a senior competition. But he made up for both in a game in which he was outstanding in midfield and picked up the only goal of a close game.

Glenn Hoddle was there to see United's England players outplay Chelsea, particularly in midfield. Paul Scholes, Nicky Butt and Phil Neville worked brilliantly to blunt the Chelsea attack all through the game.

When the chance came to score, Phil Neville showed his turn of speed. Denis Irwin passed the ball to Teddy Sheringham. He played a one-two with Andy Cole and then hit the ball over the Chelsea back line. Meanwhile Phil raced into the box to collect the ball and found himself within shooting distance. He used great control to steady himself, took aim and then sent the ball into the net with a well-judged finish.

Yet only a few moments after scoring his first goal, Phil was back in defence closing down a Chelsea attack. Which goes to prove that Alex Ferguson's team are United in name and united in play.

Of course, it's play and flexibility like that demonstrated by Phil Neville that makes United the Champions!

First published in 1998 by Manchester United Books, an imprint of
VCI, 76 Dean Street, London, W1V 5HA.
Web site: www.vci.co.uk.

Text copyright © 1998 Manchester United Books

A catalogue record for this title is available from the British Library

ISBN 0 233 99370 3
Designed by Words & Pictures Ltd
Printed in Italy

Photographs by John Peters, Action Images, Allsport,
Empics and Popperfoto

With special thanks to John Peters, Rachel Jervis, Cliff Butler
and Mike Laganis at Manchester United.